Milk and Dairy

D1715591

D.H. Dilkes

Enslow Elementary
an imprint of

Enslow Publishers, Inc.
40 Industrial Road
Box 398
Berkeley Heights, NJ 07922
USA

http://www.enslow.com

For my girls: Nicole, Jocelynn, and Devynn

Enslow Elementary, an imprint of Enslow Publishers, Inc.
Enslow Elementary® is a registered trademark of Enslow Publishers, Inc.

Library of Congress Cataloging-in-Publication Data

Dilkes, D. H.
  Milk and dairy / D.H. Dilkes.
      p. cm. — (All about good foods we eat)
  Includes bibliographical references and index.
  Summary: "Introduces dairy in everyday meals to pre-readers using repetition of words and short, simple sentences with photos and illustrations to enhance the text"—Provided by publisher.
  ISBN 978-0-7660-3924-7
  1. Milk—Juvenile literature. 2. Dairy products—Juvenile literature. I. Title.
  TX556.M5D55 2012
  641.3'7—dc23   2011015678

Paperback ISBN 978-1-59845-253-2

Printed in the United States of America
052011 Lake Book Manufacturing, Inc., Melrose Park, IL

10 9 8 7 6 5 4 3 2 1

To Our Readers: We have done our best to make sure all Internet Addresses in this book were active and appropriate when we went to press. However, the author and the publisher have no control over and assume no liability for the material available on those Internet sites or on other Web sites they may link to. Any comments or suggestions can be sent by e-mail to comments@enslow.com or to the address on the back cover.

Photo Credits: Shutterstock.com

Cover Photo: Shutterstock.com

Note to Parents and Teachers

Help pre-readers get a jumpstart on reading. These lively stories introduce simple concepts with repetition of words and short simple sentences. Photos and illustrations fill the pages with color and effectively enhance the text. Free Educator Guides are available for this series at www.enslow.com. Search for the *All About Good Foods We Eat* series name.

Warning: The foods in this book may contain ingredients to which people may be allergic, such as peanuts and milk.

Contents

Words to Know

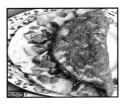  

omelet   pasta   Swiss

I like to drink milk.

I drink it with my breakfast.

I like cheese in my omelet.

I eat it for breakfast.

I have a sandwich for lunch.

I put Swiss cheese on it.

I also have a sandwich.

I like grilled cheese.

I am eating dinner.

Mac and cheese
tastes good.

I am ready for dinner.

I like cheese on my pasta.

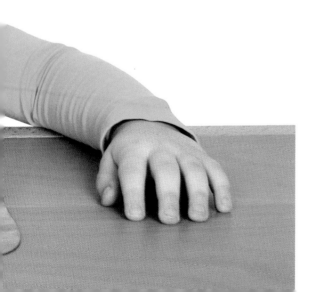

Yogurt is a good snack.

I eat it with a spoon.

I am eating a slice
of cheese.

I like it for a snack.

My baby brother likes dessert.

He is eating pudding.

Frozen yogurt is a nice treat.

I like it for dessert.

Read More

Burstein, John. *Delicious Dairy*. New York: Crabtree Pub., 2010.

Kalz, Jill. *Dairy Products*. North Mankato, Minn.: Smart Apple Media, 2003.

Web Sites

PBS Kids: *Sid the Science Kid* Mix it Up
<http://pbskids.org/sid/mixitup.html>
Help Sid create a balanced meal!

Smallstep Kids: MyPyramid Blast Off
<http://teamnutrition.usda.gov/Resources/game/BlastOff_Game.
    html>
A fun game that teaches the food pyramid.

Index

Guided Reading Level: D
Guided Reading Leveling System is based on the guidelines
recommended by Fountas and Pinnell.

Word Count: 107